Grieving In Love

By

Lora Mitchell

This book is dedicated to the many people who I have lost in the last 5 years. I won't list all of them because their names could honestly fill this book, but I will list a few.

Bishop Julian C. Jackson
Aunt Ernestine Allen
Cousin Terrel Jones
Aunt Gail Dozier
Joseph E. Harris
Sonya Porter

I love each of you and the many whose names aren't listed. You each impacted my life in ways that I have yet to fully uncover.

To my family and friends who have loved and supported me,
Thank you!

To each of you who picks up this book and reads the words within its pages,
Thank you!
May you find peace, solace, and company on your journey through your own grief.

Table of Contents

Dancing with My Grandfather	9
I Miss You As Much As I Love You	10
Requiem for a Toddler	11
Holding You Back (Letting Go)	13
I Mourn	15
Chadwick	20
An Ode to Sondheim	22
If I'm Honest	24
Pieces of Me	26
In Love & Conflict	27
Better than the One We Had	29
Whispers of Justice	31
Ugliness Crept Into Our Safe Spaces	32

Am I American First	35
DVDs	38
Death's Coming	40
How I Feel	41

7

Dancing with my grandfather

Dancing with my grandfather
Was always one of my dreams.
Like the commercials,
I'd step on his shoes
And he'd dance with me around the dance floor.
Unfortunately, this was not to be.
This was not for us.
This was but a dream.

Reality produced a memory
Of me dancing with my grandfather
Around his wheelchair
Him preparing for death
Me just being a child.

But even in the midst
Of the mist dissipating
Of this well-worn dream
Is a beautiful reality
Of my dancing with my grandfather
For life.

I Miss You As Much As I Love You

I miss you as much as I love you
Your voice I can no longer hear.
Your smile is archived in pictures
Your touch forever lost to me

I miss you as much as I love you.
Memories assault my mind.
Popping up at random times
They cue burning rivers of tears,
A kaleidoscope of emotions,
An emptiness I can't seem to shake.

I miss you as much as I love you.
Moving on is the most difficult part.
Each step feels like a betrayal
Each breath traitorous
Each moment of joy a stab in the back
Because you're not here.

And yet,
I know,
Living
Breathing
Loving
Laughing
Is the only way to honor you and stay sane.

So as much as I miss you and love you
I learn to live
Without you here.

Requiem for a Toddler

The cruelty of this world snuffed out the light of
a beautiful angel.
2-years-old
Brown skin
Curly blond hair
A smile as bright as the morning sun.
His life, now gone.

Seeing his face makes my heart break.
A little runner
Painter
Dancer
Speaker
A lively toddler
Will now rest among
The dead.

Why?
Because humans can be so cruel
Murder
Can cross the mind of a person
Adults
Can take the lives of children
Abuse
Has become a common day occurrence

How do we find light in the midst of the darkness
that surrounds us?
How do we find peace?

How do we find the courage to fight for better amidst the heartbreak?

Honestly, I don't know.
But the need is here
The time is now.

Holding You Back (Letting Go)

I knew the moment I saw his acceptance letter
There would be tears
He was perfect in every way I could think of.
Including having the brains to get into his perfect school,
On the other side of the country.
I'd barely made it into our local, state school.

I turned to him
With a smile on my face
Tears welling in my eyes
"We need to talk"
"No we don't"
He says.
So for a moment
We just hold hands
Letting them express
Words unspoken
Yet pulsing

Finally, I say it
"I'm not holding you back,
You are free."
"I don't want to be free,
I want to be whole"
He says.
"If it's meant to be,
We'll be together again.

But love is not bondage and obligation,
Love is a choice
Based on the freedom
To go.
I'm giving you the chance to one day make a real choice.
Just not today."

Before he can say anything else
To change my mind
I walked away.
Hurting like hell
But knowing I was right
To let go.

I Mourn

It is heartening and heartbreaking to see these stories of families being broken apart at the border.
It is good to see the outrage.
The tears.
The organizing.
The waking up.
It is time!

But there is a sadness that comes,
Calling to parts of me
And memories that remind me
This is America.

It's sad to see it be political.
To see people make it about
Biden
Trump
Obama
Bush
Clinton
Whoever
Negates a point that all of us need to acknowledge
This is an American problem.
We have blood on our hands.

This is a moral problem.

If splitting families is okay with you based on who is in office,
You don't have a difference in politics
You have a heart issue
You have a God issue
You have a human issue.

It is sad to be reminded this is historical.
Thinking of African and African-American families being split during and after slavery makes me weep.
Those were people.
Real families.
Real parents.
Real children.
Real lives
Forever changed.

I think of Native American families
Whose children were stolen from them.
Placed in schools meant to deplete them of who they are
Abused for using their native tongues
"Christianized",
not from the heart,
but for power
numbers,
just because.

So many people groups can speak to this experience
The Japanese think of internment camps

The Chinese the Exclusion Act

The Jewish, children turned away to return to their deaths

The Mexican, the annexing of Mexico for the creation of Texas

The LGBTQ, the splitting of their families for decades

Low-income families, improper uses of child protective services and mass incarceration.

If you really believe this is just about now and just started a few days ago,

No,

This is America.

WE HAVE BLOOD ON OUR HANDS!

It's personal.

I think of my aunts and uncles spending every family holiday trying to piece together our family tree.

Of my refusal to date in certain states

Not wanting to mistakenly marry a cousin

I look at people with my family name

Longing

Wondering,

Questioning

Do you belong to me?

Do you belong to us?

Because the splitting of families in slavery wasn't just a page in a book.

But a page out of my own family history.

It's spiritual.
It rends apart the heart of God
That His creation
Can't see all of
Her creation
As made in
Their image
God's likeness

The Indians say
Namaste
Which means
I see the God in you
And yet,
So many have difficulty
Seeing the humanity in
Eyes
Staring back at them

I don't know where to place that hurt
So I write
I cry
I rage
I tweet
I fight
I mourn
Mourn the waxing of the hearts of man
Mourn the babies crying.
Mourn for the mothers and fathers
Trying to understand

How seeking asylum
Has landed them in a new sort of
Hell.

I mourn for a nation that justifies evil
Winks at immorality
For a church that debates a truth
At the foundation of Your Word,
That You made humanity
In Your likeness and image
That we are to Love You
With all our hearts, mind, souls and strength
And love our neighbor as ourselves.
I mourn God.
I mourn Father.
I mourn.

Chadwick

Oh Chad
Sweet Chadwick
How we miss you already.

43 is too soon.
Too young.
To give you up.

Yet with 43,
You showed us who we are.
Our strength
Courage
Wisdom
Humor
Talent
Grace
Were displayed in your every role.

We adored you
Looked up to you
Recognized you
As our
Justice
Hero
Athletes
Our King.

T'challa made us feel
Special

Represented
Seen.

We cry
Mourn
And await
In Sorrow
For the day
Our time will come.

Until then
Rest well
Sleep on
We'll see you in the morning.

Ode to Sondheim

It's our turn to throw Roses for the one and only
Stephen Sondheim.

Your songs reminded us that Being Alive is only worth it,
If we do it Side-by-Side
With each other.
In a big, scary world,
You reminded us that
No One is Alone.

With our hearts in hand,
We are Sorry-Grateful
For your death.
Sorry with sorrow that we'll never hear
That laugh
That voice
That wit
On this side again.
Grateful and thankful
That you leave behind a treasure trove of
Songs
Lectures
Interviews
Memories
To remember you by.

As the Children Listen,
We pray that this bard of American
Brings new meaning, life and inspiration for
Generations to come.
May your memory not just be a blessing,
But a movement.
Sparking a Company of
Artists
Writers
Producers
Brave enough
To pick up your mantle for a fresher and braver era of storytelling.

As we try to Move On,
Wondering What We Will Do Without You,
We question
Will you be forgotten
Or seen as passe?
Not While We Are Around
To reveal
Your life and gifts
To those who will come.
While Sundays in the Park
Will never be the same
Without You,
We know that Not A Day Will Go By,
Where we won't think about you.
Until It's Our Time,
I Guess This Is Goodbye.

If I'm Honest

If I'm honest,
I'm happy and blessed,
But also,
I'm sad and depressed.
How these 2 realities can exist,
Much less the myriad of others,
Never ceases to amaze me.

There's a temptation to pretend
I'm only happy.
I'm only joyful
On Cloud 9
Enjoying joy.
I'm so grateful for
Humor
And spaces of grace and peace.
Holding on to these moments feels right.

But,
If I'm honest,
Sadness, hurt and grief
Creep in
Take residence
And demand to be respected.
They demand my attention.
They remind me
"We belong here too!"

The complexity of life

Is that,
They're right.
I don't want or need to just be
Happy
At peace
Joyous
Humorous
Blessed.

They feel good,
But are only a limited
Set of colors
In the palette of life.

Anger helps us see
Where our hurts and passions lie.
Sadness reminds us
There are things and experiences
That we still long for
Grief honors the love and memory
Of loved ones and things
That are no longer with us.
Even depression,
In all of it's numbness and apathy
Reminds us to hold on to life.
To feel the moments
To enjoy the present
Because we don't know
When things will shift
And change.

Pieces of Me

Joy here
Sadness there
Flaw here
Gift over there
Rage under the surface
Laughter bubbling over at any given moment.

Reflecting on me
I see pieces of me
Floating down the river
Of my life.

I pray for healing
And wholeness
For the pieces of me
To come together
To make up
A whole, restored
Me.

In Love & Conflict

If I didn't love you
It wouldn't hurt so bad
The break wouldn't feel so hard
The wait wouldn't feel so long.

If I didn't care
I could move on
Laughing and joking
Living and loving
Going about my daily life
Like you don't exist

But I do care
I do love you
I do miss your presence
In my life

I miss the good times
I miss the bad
I miss the advice and giggles
The jokes and heartaches
The honesty and revelations

I miss being your friend
And you being mine
I hope for the day of restoration
I mourn for the days lost
To conflict

Better Than the One We Had

Dear friend,
It's time to move on.
What we had was fun
Exciting
Nurturing
Yet toxic and dangerous

You provided me with laughs
You sat with me in dark moments
You built my confidence
Even as you wrestled to hold on to yours
I will forever be grateful
For your friendship and the times we had.

But it's time to move on.
Either away from each other
Or in a path built on
Health
Healing
Authenticity
Truth
Laughing through the pain is fine,

But why stay bound
When healing is available?

In the meantime,
I must heal for me
I must break free
In order to be whole.
I must make space for me
In order to find a place for you,
If you want it,
In a life
That's better
Than the one we had.

Whispers for Justice

Ma'Khia is her name.
Makayla is her name.
Sandra is her name.
Renisha is her name.
Rekia is her name.

These women and girls are ancestors
Way too soon.

Shot down in the prime of their lives
They now watch over us.
Whispering for justice
Whispering for truth
To prevail.

Ugliness Crept Into Our Safe Spaces

Ugliness crept into our safe spaces
And left behind tears
Mothers, fathers, lovers and friends
Weeping for loved ones gone
Heartbroken and shattered
Lives changed forever
At the end of a gun.

It crept into our spaces
And left behind screaming
Chaos ensued as dancing stopped
As books were closed
As hard decisions had to be made.
"Do I save others?"
"Do I save myself?"
"Is there a way not to die?"

Ugliness crept into our safe spaces
And left behind silence.
Once the carnage had ended
And the killers were gone,
Now there was only
The quiet
The clean-up
The shock

The pain.

Ugliness crept into our safe spaces
And left behind conversations
Two communities, previously at odds
Had to have hard talks
And speak of shared pain
The need to make our spaces
Safe again
For each other.

Ugliness crept into our safe spaces
And left behind change
Symbols of hate came down
While flags of love fly high
Marches and services carried on
In defiance
To the terror
Of these mad men
Who hoped to wrought
Fear in the hearts
Of good-willed people everywhere.
Side-by-side,
The survivors cry
"We will not be afraid."
"You will not win!"

Ugliness crept into our safe spaces
And left behind grace.

Oh sweet amazing grace.
Forgiveness and sharing
Understanding and space.
Space to grow
Space to heal
Space for beauty
To creep back into
Where ugliness once resided
Here.

Am I American First?

Am I American First?
No,
First I am human.

Flesh, blood
Sweat, tears

If only I could get you to
See me
As human

See all as human

Then maybe,
We would see
The end of the killing of
humans

But you say,
"They deserve it"

When did we give over our
Humanity?
Over to men,
To women,
To people,
Who determine
Who has the right
To breathe?

The right to live?
Life
Liberty
The Pursuit of Happiness
Or did I forget to breathe
Enough for these to apply
To me?

Am I American first?
Of course not.
The complexity of
The identity
That dwells in me
Is too deep
To be
Confined
To a flag and a pledge

Anthems and allegiances
To ideas
That don't always
Apply to me
See,
I'm one of those identities
That don't always warrant
Humanity
In the eyes
Of the law.

So what am I remaining loyal to?
My life
My breath
Or my death?

DVDS

"CDs, DVDs, come get your DVDs"

This is the cry I hear on Friday nights in parking lots in my hood.

Young men selling entertainment for the nice low price of
Milk, feeding themselves and their children
With the money from DVDs.

CDs, DVDs, come get your DVDs,
Come get your HIV,
Dying

Sweet love making leads to sweat, blood and tears
Cried in the doctor's office

The result reminds us that we're not invincible
As we watch DVDs in the dark.

Come get your DVDs,
Come get your police brutality

I wonder if Alton knew he would star in his own movie one day.
As he peddled DVDs to get shoes,
Bus passes,

Voter Ids.
I wonder did his dreams ever
Foresee the nightmare that would feature his
own death.

CDs, DVDs, come get your DVDs,
And see.

Death's Coming

My heart is trying to accept something my mind already knows.
Death approaches.

My heart is crying
Confused
Screaming
Wailing

My mind wants to stay calm,
Be in control,
Prepare my body for the shock.
My soul knows this is the time for faith.

No matter the outcome
God is in control
She knows best.
They will not leave me during this time,
He's here now.

God's here in the midst of the confusion and mayhem.
She's here in the midst of the calm and control.
They're here in the midst of faith and fear.
He's here. She's here. God is here.

How I Feel

Angry.
Angry at the lack of caring for
Black bodies
Trans bodies
Gay bodies
Bodies overseas.
The silence is deafening.
The few voices that make it out are
Angry
Passionate
Not Understanding

Sad.
Sad to live in a world in which crimes against
children are justified.
Violence
Rape
Murder
They are okay
As long as it doesn't happen to
My children
The parents who cry out are shamed.
The children who speak are silenced.
Those who support them, called thugs.
Lord, what kind of world do we live in?

Frustrated.
Frustrated at the now-and-not-yet of

Progress
Change
Justice.
One guilty verdict here.
2 not-guilty verdicts there.
One acknowledgement here
One misrepresentation there.
He gives clemency to 22,
Calls angry teens
Thugs and criminals
Where is the lever?
The one that will pour out
Love
Faith
Truth
Justice for all
Where's the committee we can appeal to?
To see people treated like human beings.

Enraged.
Enraged that it feels like we're
Living in hell down here.
They tell me there's another hell for those who don't believe.
How much worse can it get
To be the living epitome of the conscious
The world chooses to
Ignore
Silence
Bury?

How many more mothers have to cry
Before there will be some relief?
How many people have to die
Before the believers and healers
Wake up?
How much longer can we take this
Before we explode?
How much longer before
The blind face the ugly truth
That compliance
Cannot save you
From the murderous
Hands of hate?

www.ingramcontent.com/pod-product-compliance
Lightning Source LLC
LaVergne TN
LVHW051529070426
835507LV00023B/3379